MORE HOMONYMS

steak and stake and other
WORDS THAT SOUND THE SAME
but look as different as
chili and chilly

MORE
HOMONYMS

ILLUSTRATED
BY
JOAN HANSON

Published by
Lerner Publications Company
Minneapolis, Minnesota

FOR
AMEAL

International Standard Book Number: 0-8225-0287-9
Library of Congress Catalog Card Number: 73-11971

Third Printing 1975

hom·o·nym (HAHM-uh-nim) A word that sounds the same as another word but has a different spelling and meaning. These words are homonyms: *see* and *sea*; *made* and *maid*; *dear* and *deer*.

Chili

Chilly

Steak

Stake

Board

Bored

Whale

Wail

Raise

Rays

Wait

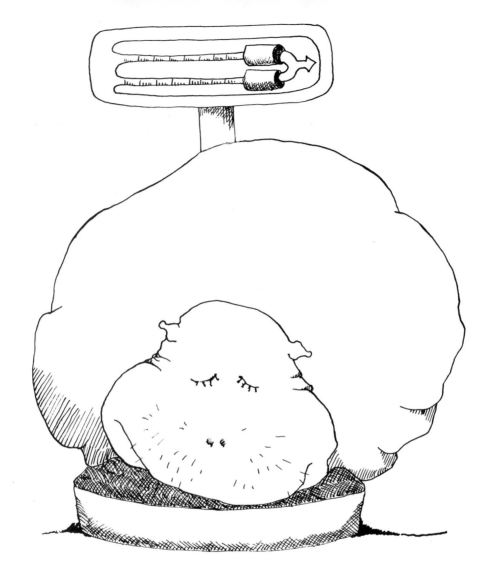

Weight

Might

Mite

Whole

Hole

Sell

Cell

Horse

Hoarse

Toe

Tow

Steel

Steal

Fairy

Ferry

BOOKS IN THIS SERIES

ANTONYMS
hot and cold and other
WORDS THAT ARE DIFFERENT
as night and day

MORE ANTONYMS
wild and tame and other ·
WORDS THAT ARE AS DIFFERENT IN MEANING
as work and play

HOMONYMS
hair and hare and other
WORDS THAT SOUND THE SAME
but look as different as bear and bare

MORE HOMONYMS
steak and stake and other
WORDS THAT SOUND THE SAME
but look as different as chili and chilly

HOMOGRAPHS
bow and bow and other
WORDS THAT LOOK THE SAME
but sound as different as sow and sow

HOMOGRAPHIC HOMOPHONES
fly and fly and other
WORDS THAT LOOK AND SOUND THE SAME
but are as different in meaning as bat and bat

British-American SYNONYMS
french fries and chips and other
WORDS THAT MEAN THE SAME THING
but look and sound
as different as truck and lorry

MORE SYNONYMS
shout and yell and other
WORDS THAT MEAN THE SAME THING
but look and sound
as different as loud and noisy

We specialize in producing quality books for
young people. For a complete list please write

LERNER PUBLICATIONS COMPANY
241 First Avenue North, Minneapolis, Minnesota 55401